Festivals of the World

INDIA

D0993597

Heinemann

First published in Great Britain by
Heinemann Library
Halley Court, Jordan Hill, Oxford
OX2 8EJ
a division of Reed Educational and
Professional Publishing Ltd.

OXFORD   FLORENCE   PRAGUE
MADRID   ATHENS   MELBOURNE
AUCKLAND   KUALA LUMPUR
SINGAPORE   TOKYO   IBADAN
NAIROBI   KAMPALA
JOHANNESBURG   GABORONE
PORTSMOUTH NH   CHICAGO
MEXICO CITY   SAO PAULO

First edition © TIMES EDITIONS
PTE LTD 1997
This edition © Reed Educational
and Professional Publishing Ltd
1997

Written by Falaq Kagda
Designed by Hasnah Mohd Esa
and Celia Floyd
Printed in Singapore

01 00 99 98 97
10 9 8 7 6 5 4 3 2 1

ISBN 0 431 05492 4 (hardback)
ISBN 0 431 05493 2 (paperback)

British Library Cataloguing in
Publication Data

Kagda, Falaq
   India. – (Festivals of the world)
   1. Festivals – India – Juvenile
     literature
   I. Title
   394.2'6954

Contents

It's festival time . . .

Whatever your religion, whoever you are, there are plenty of festivals for you in India. Whether you're Muslim or Sikh or Christian, farmer or merchant, there's a festival specially for you. And with every festival, there's a **mela** [*MAY-la*] that goes with it (that means 'fair' in **Hindi**). Come along, take a ride on the big wheel, go on an elephant ride (or do you prefer camels?) and buy some pretty jewellery. Put on your best clothes, because it's festival time in India . . .

Where's India?

India takes up most of South Asia. It is a huge country and more crowded than almost anywhere else in the world. One person in every six people on earth lives in India. The country has everything from the highest mountain range in the world on its northern border to hot tropical jungles in the south. At the heart of India are the Indus and Ganges rivers, which bring life to the plains around them. The Ganges is sacred to Indians. The capital is New Delhi. India also has other very large and crowded cities, like Calcutta and Bombay.

Who are the Indians?

There are many different kinds of people in India. Those in the south are smaller and darker than those in the north, and there are many variations in between. That is because long ago **Caucasians** moved from Persia into India, where the dark-skinned **Dravidians** were already living. Over the centuries, they have mixed and created people of many different colours and features. Indians speak a variety of languages and have widely different customs. Most Indians are Hindus, but there are also many Muslims, Sikhs, Christians, Buddhists and Jains.

A smiling Indian girl wears a garland of flowers, ready to go to a festival.

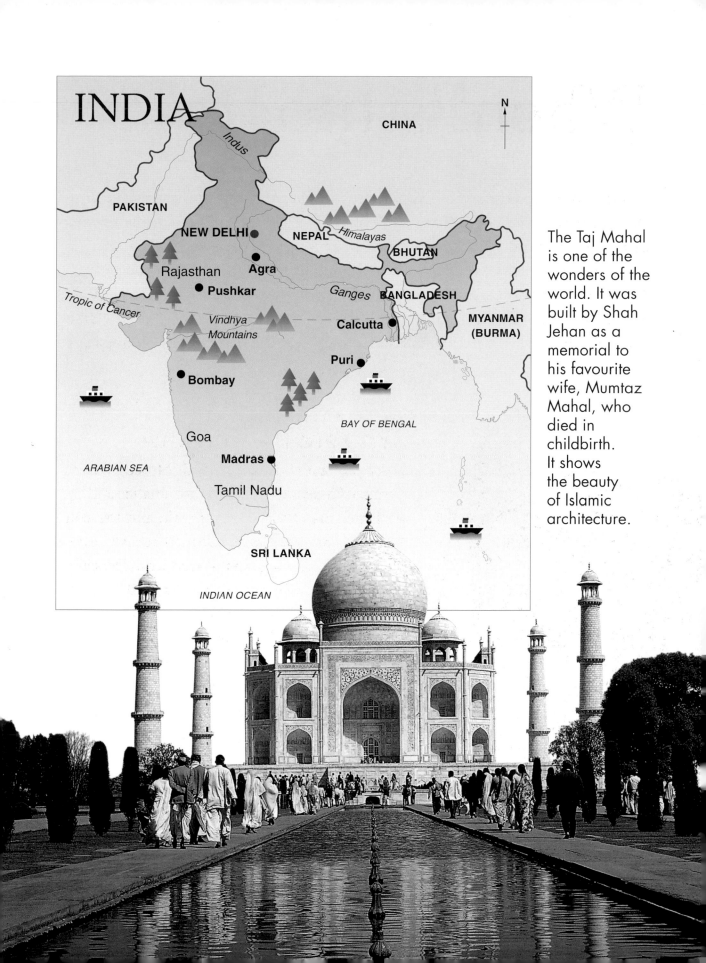

INDIA

CHINA

N

Indus

PAKISTAN

NEW DELHI

NEPAL

Himalayas

BHUTAN

Rajasthan

Agra

Pushkar

Ganges

BANGLADESH

Tropic of Cancer

Vindhya
Mountains

Calcutta

MYANMAR
(BURMA)

Puri

Bombay

BAY OF BENGAL

Goa

ARABIAN SEA

Madras

Tamil Nadu

SRI LANKA

INDIAN OCEAN

The Taj Mahal
is one of the
wonders of the
world. It was
built by Shah
Jehan as a
memorial to
his favourite
wife, Mumtaz
Mahal, who
died in
childbirth.
It shows
the beauty
of Islamic
architecture.

When's the *Mela?*

Indians use three different calendars. Hindu festivals follow a special **lunar** calendar. This calendar follows the phases of the moon. The dates of these festivals change from year to year on the Gregorian calendar (that's the one you're probably used to). Muslims follow a different lunar calendar. Their festivals move back eleven days every year, so they aren't even in the same season from year to year.

SPRING

- *Basant* – For this celebration of spring, people wear something yellow. Often there are kite-flying competitions.
- *Mahavir Jayanti* – Celebrates the birthday of Vardhamana Mahavira, who started the Jain religion. Jains come from all over to visit their shrine at Gimar. ● *Holi* ● *Pooram*
- *Baisakhi* – Sikhs celebrate the New Year at this time. They have a big meal together at the temple, then dance the bhangra in the streets in the evening (look at page eleven to see the *bhangra*).

Want some colour in your life? Join me for Holi on page 16.

SUMMER

- *Ratha Jatra* (The Chariot Festival) Images of Krishna and his family are dragged through the streets of Puri on huge chariots. It takes 4,000 people to pull one of these chariots.
- **Independence Day**
- *Raksha Bandhan*
- *Naag Panchami*

Come monkey around with the animals on page 20.

AUTUMN

- *Dassehra* – The festival of the mother goddess, Durga. Statues of Durga are carried to the Ganges River and thrown in.
- *Divali* • *Pushkar Mela*
- **Gandhi Jayanta** – Celebrates Gandhi's birthday (2 October).

The Republic Day celebration starts on page 8.

WINTER

- *Guru Nanak Jayanti* – Sikhs celebrate the birthday of Guru Nanak, who started Sikhism. • **Republic Day** • *Ponggal*
- **Carnival** – Christians in Goa celebrate *Carnival* with a traditional red-and-black dance, when they wear only red and black.

Muslim holidays

- *Muharram* – The anniversary of the day when Prophet Muhammad left for Medina. There are processions in honour of Husain, the Prophet's grandson, who was killed on this day.
- *Id-ul-Fitr* – Marks the end of the fasting month of Ramadhan. People wear new clothes and have big feasts.
- *Id-ul-Adha* – People kill a sheep to eat in memory of Ibrahim's willingness to sacrifice his son Isma'il.

7

Republic Day

Have you ever seen a National Day parade with elephants painted in bright colours? If you haven't, come to New Delhi on 26 January for Republic Day! While elephants and camels march down the street, aeroplanes put on an air show. There are people in all kinds of dress from the different regions of India. Dancers show off the dances of their region. What a show it is to see all these peoples come together to celebrate their country!

Come to the parade

On a low hill in the centre of New Delhi is a red sandstone palace where the president of India lives. Below is a grassy park. This is where the Republic Day parade takes place. Long rows of wooden benches are set up. In the centre is a seat under a gold umbrella. The president sits there to review the parade. Troops of horsemen ride past wearing red coats and gold turbans. Next come the elephants, their trunks painted with flowers. Soldiers and sailors, boy scouts and girl guides, and patriotic groups march past in their uniforms. Then come the floats representing the states of the Republic of India. Each is brightly decorated to show off the best of its state.

This elephant is decorated to march in the parade. National heroes have the honour of riding on the elephants.

What is Republic Day?

Indians have two independence days. Republic Day celebrates the day in 1926 when Indians declared their independence from Great Britain. Independence Day celebrates the day 20 years later when the British turned over power to Pandit Jawaharlal Nehru, India's first prime minister. On Independence Day, the president makes a speech. But the real show takes place on Republic Day, when the weather is cool enough to sit outside and watch a parade.

A corps of women soldiers march in perfect form.

The camel corps from the desert region of Bikaner is one of the high points of the parade.

Independence

Many years ago, India was a colony of Great Britain, but Indians wanted to run their own country. They thought the British were using India to make themselves rich, while Indians stayed very poor. How could the Indians force the British to leave?

A great man

Mohandas K. Gandhi was a leader of the Indian struggle for independence. People call him Mahatma Gandhi. *Mahatma* means 'Great Soul'. He believed that it was wrong to kill anyone. He thought the best way to make the British leave was to refuse to obey unfair laws. He called this 'passive resistance'.

Make your own salt

When the British put an expensive tax on salt, Gandhi announced he was going to make salt himself. He started walking to the sea, which was 240 km away. As he walked, people joined him. Finally there were thousands of people marching. When people saw this, they realized that the British couldn't stop them from making salt. After many demonstrations like this one, the British were forced to leave.

When he was young Gandhi wore trousers and shirts, but later he wanted to be closer to the common people of India, so he started to dress like a simple farmer. He also learned how to spin yarn and wore hand-woven clothes. People loved him because he shared the life of the simple people.

Dancers come from all parts of the country to represent their local area. Here a troupe of Sikhs dance the **bhangra** in the parade. Sikh men never cut their hair and cover it with a turban as a mark of their religion.

Let's dance

After Republic Day comes a two-day festival of music and dance. India has its own forms of music and dance that go back thousands of years and are admired all over the world. *Baharat Nhatyam* and *Kathak* are two types of traditional dance. *Kathak* dancers wear bands with rows of bells on their ankles. They make a rhythm with the bells as they move.

India is famous for its beautiful *sitar* music. The *sitar* is a large stringed instrument that makes a sound very different from any other instrument. Ravi Shankar is a famous *sitar* player. With the *sitar* you are likely to hear the **tabla**, a kind of Indian drum. Zakir Hussain is a popular *tabla* player.

Indian dance was at first a way of worshipping the gods. Most dances tell a story about gods or heroes.

Divali

It's late autumn in India, and the long nights are dark as the moon comes to the end of its monthly cycle. On the last days of *Ashwin* (that's the Hindu month that falls in October or November), rows of small, flickering clay lamps appear in doorways, on window-ledges, even lighting the outlines of towering government buildings. These are the lights of *Divali* [*dee-WAL-ly*], the Festival of Lights. *Divali* is dedicated to Lakshmi, the Hindu goddess of wealth and beauty. During the five days of *Divali*, Lakshmi visits houses and shops that are clean and well lit. And with her she brings wealth and good fortune, so all of India is lit up to invite her in.

A new beginning

To get ready for *Divali*, Indians buy new clothes and clean and maybe paint the house. Shopkeepers start a new year, and everyone pays off what they owe. *Divali* is a time to start afresh, with the hope that Lakshmi will bring better fortune in the next year. Hindus go to their temples to honour the gods. Then they come home and eat special meals. Later they visit family and friends, bringing gifts of sweets. It is traditional to give sweets at *Divali*. Do you want to know how *Divali* started? Listen to a story . . .

A Hindu goddess is decorated for *Divali*. Hindu gods and goddesses often have several sets of arms to show how powerful they are.

Here are rows and rows of sweets, flowers and fruit laid out as offerings to the gods.

The Demon of Filth

Once there was a very dirty demon named Naraka or the Demon of Filth. He never took a bath or cleaned his house. He kidnapped young girls including Lakshmi and took them to live in his dirty house.

Krishna (one of the most popular Hindu gods) fought with Naraka and won. As Naraka was dying, he felt sorry that he had made people unhappy. He asked Krishna to make the anniversary of his death a day when people would be happy. That day is *Divali*. People celebrate by taking scented baths and dressing up in new clothes.

Divali lights on a street in Rajasthan.

The lights of goodness

Divali means 'row of lights'. On the long, dark nights of *Divali*, the lamps remind people that goodness and wisdom are stronger than the forces of darkness. There are many stories that people tell about *Divali*, but all of them are about the triumph of good over evil. Here's another story about the victory of good over evil that is part of the *Divali* tradition.

Lights invite Lakshmi to bring good fortune. A tradition for young girls is to set *Divali* lamps afloat in the river. If the light burns as long as its owner can see it, she will have good luck in the next year.

One of the stories that goes with *Divali* is that of the hero Rama's return to his kingdom. Here people use dance to tell the story of Rama's adventures.

Think about this

Hindus believe in one god that is in all living things. But they believe that it is too hard for people to understand this god, so they use a lot of other gods to show the different sides of god. The main three are called Brahma (the Creator), Vishnu (the Protector) and Shiva (the Destroyer).

Rama comes home

Many Indian festivals celebrate several things at once. *Divali* lights also remind Hindus of the story of Rama's return to his kingdom. According to the story, Rama, an Indian hero, was unfairly sent away from his kingdom. Then the demon Ravenna kidnapped Rama's wife. Rama spent fourteen years searching for her. Finally there was a big battle, and Rama destroyed Ravenna. When Rama returned to his kingdom, the people lit lamps to guide him back.

During the holiday of *Dassehra* [*duh-SHEH-rah*], which comes just before *Divali*, people put up giant statues of Ravenna. At the end of the festival, they put firecrackers inside the statues and set them on fire. *Divali* is when Rama returned to his kingdom. On that night, Indians light lamps to celebrate Rama's return.

Here are statues of the evil Ravenna and his son and brother ready to be set on fire.

Holi

If you're in India one day in March and someone comes up and throws red powder all over you, don't be surprised. This is *Holi*, and on *Holi* people walk around yelling, *'Holi hai, Holi hai'* and throwing coloured water or powder at anyone they see, even if it's their teacher or the mayor of their town. During *Holi* everyone is equal and everything is forgiven. The important things are *'rang, ras, and rag'* (colour, dance and song). So get in on the fun, throw a little powder and join in the dancing and singing. This is the Festival of Colours. All the rules are off.

Some people use bicycle pumps to squirt red, yellow and green liquid over everyone.

A fun time

On the first night, the young men and boys make a huge bonfire. Men and boys dance around the fire, sometimes jumping through it. Food that has just been harvested is put on the fire as an offering. The next morning the fun begins. Besides the colour throwing, there are huge fairs and circuses. People forget whatever arguments they have had with anyone. It's a time to start afresh.

Powders of different colours are offered for sale on the streets. These colours usually wash out of clothes without too much trouble.

Beating up the boys

Near Delhi, the women of one village pretend to have a fight with the men of a nearby village. The women carry long bamboo poles. They try to hit the men with the poles. The men carry leather shields. They dodge through the crowds, trying to escape the women. When the women get tired, the men shout insults to get them started again. It's all in fun and everyone has a good laugh.

Although *Holi* is a Hindu festival, it is a big carnival that people of all religions join in. A nice thing about *Holi* is the way it breaks down barriers.

In the evening, people change into clean clothes. They get together in public squares to eat, drink, talk and watch local folk dances.

The *Holi* story

There are many stories about *Holi* in different parts of the country. The best known is about a young prince named Prahlada. Prahlada worshipped the god Vishnu, but his father wanted everyone to worship him. He asked his evil daughter, Holika, to help him punish Prahlada when he refused. Holika had the power to walk through fire without being burned. She carried Prahlada into a bonfire. People heard terrible screams but finally, Prahlada walked out alone. His faith had protected him, while the evil Holika burned. That's why there are bonfires for *Holi* today.

Think about this

Does your family do a spring clean? At one time, rubbish was taken out and burned in bonfires during spring festivals. This was a way of getting rid of the remains of winter and starting afresh. In Britain, people still have a day of practical jokes once a year – do you know when it is? (Hint: It's close to the same time as *Holi*.)

This is a painting of Krishna. When he was a boy, he was very mischievous. He stole milk from the milkmaids. To get him back, they threw coloured powder at him. That is why people throw colours at each other during *Holi*.

Celebrating springtime

Holi is also very much like many other spring festivals around the world. It is a time to be happy that winter is over and food is starting to grow again. In India, the spring wheat harvest comes round at this time of the year.

For the beasts

Animals have an important place in Indian life, and Indians have a great respect for them. There are several festivals in India that are for the animals, to thank them for their help during the year. For *Pooram*, elephants wear gold head ornaments in a parade. The men riding on the elephants carry brightly coloured umbrellas and peacock feather whisks. *Naag Panchami* is the Festival of the Snakes. People give milk and flowers to snakes that live in the temples. A special event for camels is the *Pushkar Mela*.

Come to the fair

Melas, or village fairs, accompany many religious festivals in India. There are also special *melas* where people come to trade animals. People come to the fair from all around, dressed in their best clothes. Stalls sell everything you can imagine, from pots and pans to jewellery for the women, fruits and vegetables and cows and horses (or camels!). There are magic shows, street dances, puppet shows and circuses. No matter what their religion, everyone enjoys a *mela*!

A Rajasthani couple take a ride around the fair on their camel. People from Rajasthan wear traditional clothes different from those in other parts of India. Women often wear nose rings, like this woman.

The camels visit Pushkar

A camel shows off the tricks it is able to do.

Once a year, the little town of Pushkar in Rajasthan (find it on the map on page 5) comes alive with the biggest camel fair anywhere. People come from all around to trade camels and enjoy the fair. There are camel races and camel beauty contests and singing and dancing. Merchants sell everything a camel needs, like colourful saddles and embroidered cloth covers with little mirrors. In the evening, thousands of campfires light up the desert night.

At the full moon, people take a dip in Pushkar Lake. The lake is sacred to Hindus.

Ponggal

Hindus believe cows are very special animals, so they don't kill them. In Tamil Nadu, a province in southern India, they have a festival where they honour the cows. It's called *Ponggal*, which is also the name of a sweet made from rice, milk and brown sugar. Part of the *Ponggal* Festival is to make *Ponggal* sweets and offer them to the gods. *Ponggal* celebrates the rice harvest, so they use the new rice they have just picked. After they have offered it to the gods, everyone shares the sweets. They also offer the gods clay statues of horses to thank them for sending rain for the growing rice.

Women have their hair decorated with flower garlands for the festival.

For *Ponggal* people like to decorate their front steps. They take powdered chalk or coloured rice flour and paint designs on the tiles. These are called **Rangoli designs**.

Thanks to the cows

On the third day of *Ponggal*, it's time to thank the cows. The men and boys take the cows out and give them a good bath. Then they paint their horns. Blue and gold are favourite colours. They hang garlands of flowers around their necks and put bright feathers in their hair. Often there are parades and music for the cows. They are even allowed to eat some of the *Ponggal*, too.

Let's play tag

At the end of the day, people have bullfights. But they don't kill the bull like people do in some other countries. In India, they put a packet of money between the horns of the bull and garlands of money around its neck. Then men try to snatch the money away. Sometimes it's rather dangerous, but only for the men.

A bull is dressed in his festival best for *Ponggal*.

23

Raksha Bandhan

There is no Mothers' Day or Fathers' Day in India, but there is a day for brothers and sisters. It is called *Raksha Bandhan*. On this day, sisters tie a bracelet called a **rakhi** [*RAH-kee*] around their brother's wrist. The *rakhi* is supposed to protect the brother from anything bad that might happen in the next year. She puts a dot of red powder on his forehead and gives him sweets. In return, a brother promises to care for his sister and gives her a present.

Special friends

Even after they've grown up, women give *rakhi* to their brothers and make them sweets. In return, a man might give his sister a new sari. It is a way of saying that even if they argue sometimes, they will always care for each other. Sometimes women 'adopt' a brother for *Raksha Bandhan*. This could be a friend they feel especially close to. They then become '*Rakhi* brother' and '*Rakhi* sister'.

Often on *Raksha Bandhan*, young men spend the day parading around in the streets, showing off their *rakhi*. It is a great honour to receive a *rakhi*, since it shows that someone cares greatly for you.

This little girl is tying a *rakhi* on her baby brother. In return, he gives her some fruit and money.

Things for you to do

If you were in India at festival time, you might want to play a game. How about *Pachisi*? *Pachisi* [*pah-CHEE-see*] has been played in India for hundreds of years. Indians still enjoy a good game of *Pachisi* today. Two, three or four people can play. Each person will need some kind of marker, either yellow, red, blue or green. You will also need a dice that is white on two sides and yellow, red, blue and green on the other four sides. Use the playing board on the next page. The object is to move all the way around the board and then up the diagonal strip from your home square to the star in the centre.

How to play *Pachisi*

Put your marker in the corner of the board marked with your colour. Get someone to throw the dice until a colour comes up. The person with that colour begins. Throw the dice. If it comes up the same colour as your marker, move one space anticlockwise and throw again. If it comes up white, don't move but throw again. If any other colour comes up, your turn is over. The person on your right is next. Play continues in this way. The first person to get to the centre wins.

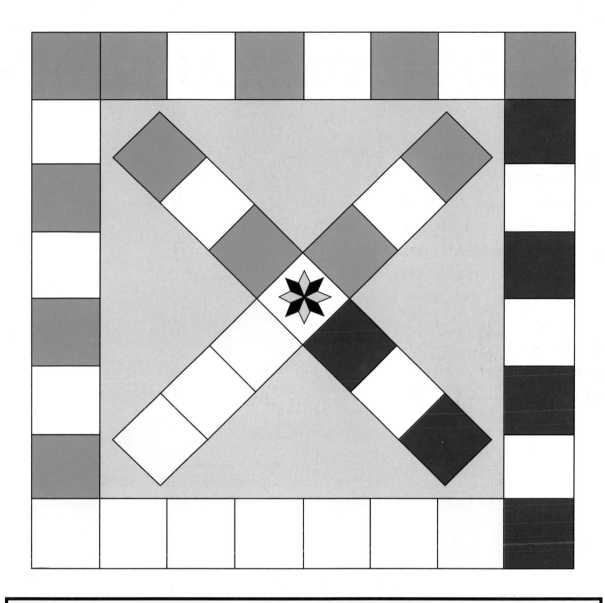

Things to look for in your library

Heinemann Stories from World Religions Heinemann Educational 1995

World of Festivals: Ramadan and Eid-ul Fitr Catherine Chambers, Evans 1996

The World of Festivals Philip Steele, Macdonald Young Books 1996

Season Festivals: Autumn/Winter/Spring/Summer Wayland 1990

I Come from India Anita Ganeri, Franklin Watts 1995

World Focus: India Amanda Barker, Heinemann Library 1994

Celebrate: Hindu Festivals Dilip Kadodwala & Paul Gateshill, Heinemann Publishers 1995

Discovering Religions: Hinduism Sue Penney, Heinemann Library 1995

Discovering Sacred Texts: The Hindu Scriptures V.P. (Hemant) Kantikar, Heinemann Library 1995

World Religions: Hinduism Dilip Kadodwala, Wayland 1995

Make a *Divali* lamp

You can make your own *Divali* lamp to light your house at *Divali*. Use the kind of clay that hardens by itself unless you know someone with a kiln who can fire it for you. Real *Divali* lamps are filled with oil. Then a wick is put in and lit. We use a candle to be safer.

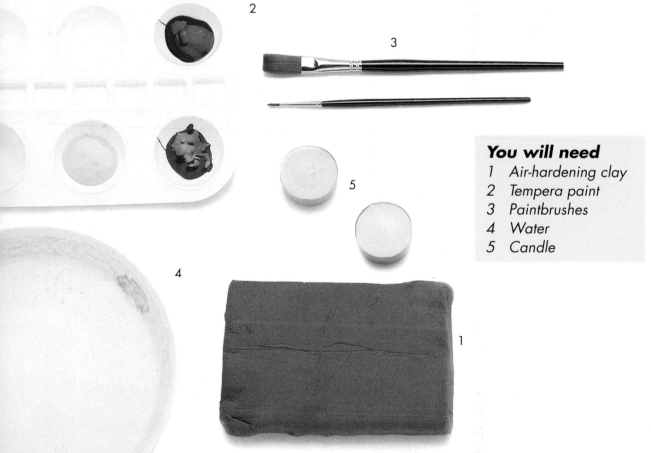

You will need
1 Air-hardening clay
2 Tempera paint
3 Paintbrushes
4 Water
5 Candle

1 Break off a handful of clay and roll it into a ball. Knead it well to make it soft enough to work with. Wet the clay from time to time as you work to keep it from drying out.

2 Mould the clay into a lamp shape by hollowing out a well in the ball. Keep working the clay until the sides are the right thickness. Keep the clay thick around the edge to form a lip. Make the bottom flat so it will sit steady. When your lamp looks the way you want it, set it aside to dry.

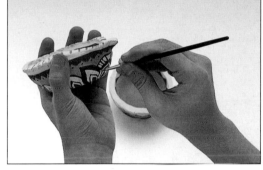

3 When your lamp has dried completely, it's time to paint it. Use bright colours to make it look nice and bright. You can put some designs on the inside, too. After the paint has dried, put a candle inside and you've finished!

Make *Burfi*

Here is a simple kind of Indian sweet. Try making *burfi* for *Divali*. There are many different kinds of *burfi* made with different kinds of nuts and flours. After you've tried your own, look for a shop that sells Indian snacks and sample some other kinds. You're sure to like them!

You will need

1 0.5 kilogram raw cashews
2 Blender
3 1 cup sweetened condensed milk
4 Butter
5 Pastry brush
6 1 teaspoon flour
7 Measuring spoons
8 Small saucepan
9 Frying pan
10 Baking tray
11 Wooden spoon
12 Knife

1 Put the cashews in a frying pan and cook them over a low heat, stirring constantly, until they are golden brown. Be careful not to burn them!

2 Grind the roasted cashews. You can use a blender or crush them with a rolling pin.

3 Mix half the ground cashews, the condensed milk and the flour in a saucepan. Cook the mixture for a few minutes until it is almost solid.

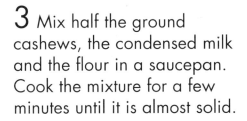

4 Grease the baking tray with the butter. Press the cashew mixture into the greased pan. Pour the remaining cashews over the top and press them into the mixture. Let it cool and then cut into squares.

Glossary

Baharat Nhatyam	*a traditional dance of India*
bhangra	*a folkdance performed by Sikh men at Baisakhi*
Kathak	*a traditional Indian dance using bells around the ankles*
Caucasians	*white people who settled in India*
Dravidians	*dark-skinned people who lived in India long ago*
Hindi	*the official language of northern India*
lunar	*following the phases of the moon*
mahatma	*a title of respect meaning 'Great Soul'*
mela	*a fair*
rakhi	*a bracelet given to brothers on Raksha Bandhan*
Rangoli designs	*designs drawn on the doorstep with chalk or coloured flour*
sitar	*an Indian stringed instrument with a long neck*
tabla	*a pair of drums of different sizes used in Indian music*
vegetarian	*someone who eats no meat or fish*

Index